ALL THE SPORTS STORIES IN THIS BOOK
ARE ABSOLUTELY TRUE—WHICH MAKES
THEM EVEN FUNNIER!

Dave Smith, a wide receiver for the Pittsburgh
Steelers, caught a pass and ran all the way—a play
covering 60 yards! Unfortunately, it should have
covered 65 yards. Smith was so excited, that he
spiked the ball before he crossed the goal line!

BASKETBALL BASEBALL FOOTBALL

SOCCER TENNIS BOXING SKIING

RUNNING GOLF SWIMMING

AND MORE!

ENCYCLOPEDIA BROWN'S
BOOK OF
WACKY SPORTS

Bantam Skylark Books by Donald J. Sobol
Ask your bookseller for the books you have missed

#1 ENCYCLOPEDIA BROWN BOY DETECTIVE

#2 ENCYCLOPEDIA BROWN AND THE CASE OF THE SECRET PITCH

#3 ENCYCLOPEDIA BROWN FINDS THE CLUES

#4 ENCYCLOPEDIA BROWN GETS HIS MAN

#6 ENCYCLOPEDIA BROWN KEEPS THE PEACE

#7 ENCYCLOPEDIA BROWN SAVES THE DAY

#8 ENCYCLOPEDIA BROWN TRACKS THEM DOWN

#9 ENCYCLOPEDIA BROWN SHOWS THE WAY

#10 ENCYCLOPEDIA BROWN TAKES THE CASE

#13 ENCYCLOPEDIA BROWN AND THE CASE OF THE MIDNIGHT VISITOR

ENCYCLOPEDIA BROWN'S BOOK OF WACKY CRIMES

ENCYCLOPEDIA BROWN'S BOOK OF WACKY SPIES

ENCYCLOPEDIA BROWN'S BOOK OF WACKY SPORTS

Encyclopedia Brown's Book of Wacky
SPORTS

DONALD J. SOBOL

Encyclopedia Brown's Book of Wacky SPORTS

Illustrated by Ted Enik

A BANTAM SKYLARK BOOK®
TORONTO • NEW YORK • LONDON • SYDNEY • AUCKLAND

RL 6, 008–012

ENCYCLOPEDIA BROWN'S BOOK OF WACKY SPORTS
A Bantam Skylark Book / November 1984

PRINTING HISTORY
William Morrow edition published September 1984.

*Skylark Books is a registered trademark of Bantam Books, Inc.
Registered in U.S. Patent and Trademark Offices and elsewhere.*

ISBN 0-553-15269-6

Published simultaneously in the United States and Canada

---

*Bantam Books are published by Bantam Books, Inc. Its trademark, consisting of
the words "Bantam Books" and the portrayal of a rooster, is Registered in U.S.
Patent and Trademark Office and in other countries. Marca Registrada. Bantam
Books, Inc., 666 Fifth Avenue, New York, New York 10103.*

PRINTED IN THE UNITED STATES OF AMERICA

O   0 9 8 7 6 5 4 3 2

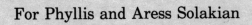

For Phyllis and Aress Solakian

Acknowledgments

In compiling this book, I received generous help from near and far. I wish to express my gratitude to:

Warren Emmery of Pasadena, Frank Pepito of Anaheim, and Luke Phillips of Monterey, California; John Barantovich, Lin Dunn, Bob Kearney, George Pearson, Cecy and Dick Rowen of Miami, and Mary Magers of Pompono Beach, Florida; Wayne Minshaw of Atlanta, Georgia; Tom Bailey and Rita Bowen of Birmingham, Alabama, and Jeff Hittler of Indianapolis, Indiana; Walter Gutowski of Baltimore, and John Meyers of Lonaconing, Maryland; Con Marshall of Chadron, Nebraska; Jim Hazlett of Union, New Jersey; Clive Gammon, Colin Reed, and Gary Zolnik of New York City, and John Manzi of Monticello, New York; Harold Ellen of Pembroke, North Carolina; Fred Gibson of The Palains, Ohio; Jim Wills of Chelsea, Hazel Clingan and Juanita Richardson of Nowata, Monteray Nelson of Oklahoma City, and Eva Sigler of Tahlequah, Oklahoma; Jerry Peacock of Huntington, Oregon; Gary Adams of Iva, South Carolina; Rebekah Harris and Edgar Miller of Chattanooga, and Betty Robinson of Ooltewah, Tennessee; Burton Hawkins of Arlington, and Spec Gammon of College Station, Texas; Gary Wright of Kirkland, Washington; Robert Davids of Washington, D.C.; John Allowat and James Jackson of Shinnston, Gregory Cartwright of Grafton, Robert Earle of Weston, J. M. Evancho and E. R. Slack of New Cumberland, Cecil Highland, Jr., of Clarksburg, Doug Huff of Wheeling, David Lowe of McConnelsville, Robert Munn and Jack Reese of Morgantown, and John Veasey of Fairmont, West Virginia; and George Chryst of Platteville, Wisconsin.

D. J. S.

Contents

Introduction   1

I.   Hoop-de-dos and Don'ts (Basketball)   5

II.   Diamond Dillies (Baseball)   24

III.   Huddling, Muddling, and
Befuddling (Football)   46

IV.   Fabulous Fistivities (Boxing)   80

V.   Razzle-Dazzle Roundup (Other Sports)   92

Introduction

Encyclopedia Brown had sprained his ankle on Thursday when he missed a lay-up.

Since then he could get around well enough to run his detective agency, located in the family garage, but it would be another week or more before he could again play summer basketball with the Woodchucks.

He limped to the front of the garage and took down his business sign. It was nearly five o'clock; office hours were over. Any minute Sally Kimball, his junior partner, and the rest of the Woodchucks would be returning from a game against the South Side Rattlers.

"The Woodchucks will do better without me," Encyclopedia thought gloomily. "They might even win."

He had just finished straightening up his desk when the Woodchucks trooped in. Sally entered first, followed by Charlie Stewart, Aress "Hook Shot" Martin, Chester Jenkins, and Fangs Liverright. They looked stunned.

"We got beat in the last second, twenty to nineteen," Sally said in disgust.

"What a game," moaned Chester. "I'm still in shock."

"You wouldn't believe what happened if we told you," Hook Shot said. "I don't believe it myself, and I was there."

"Tell me," Encyclopedia said. "I can take it."

"Those Rattlers didn't score a point from the floor," Hook Shot said. "All their points came on free throws. And still they won."

Fangs, who had been staring at his feet, raised his head and said, "We were leading with four seconds to go. They threw the ball the length of the court, hoping for a lucky basket. Instead, it struck their center."

"I had him covered every step," Charlie put in.

"So how did the Rattlers score?" Encyclopedia asked.

"The throw," Fangs answered painfully, "bounced off their center's forehead and went in for the winning two points."

"Unbelievable," groaned Chester. "Things like that just don't happen in a game."

"Oh, they've happened before," Encyclopedia said sympathetically.

"Where?" Chester demanded.

"Out in Iowa," replied Encyclopedia, "Jamaica High School defeated Bayard High, twenty-five to sixteen, and all Jamaica's points came on free throws. And in

Minnesota, a player for St. Cloud High zipped a pass to a teammate. The ball glanced off his head and went through the hoop. But it didn't help. St. Cloud lost by twelve points."

"Encyclopedia, are you making this up?" Sally exclaimed.

"Nope," replied the boy detective. He went to a shelf on the back wall of the garage and took down a large green scrapbook.

"I've been collecting stories of wacky things that have happened in sports," he said.

He laid the scrapbook on his desk and opened it. The Woodchucks crowded around. They began to read. . . .

I.

Hoop-de-dos
and Don'ts
(Basketball)

Once is enough. Weirton High School in West Virginia needed a suitable attraction to mark the opening of its new gymnasium on February 7, 1918.

Weirton's basketball coach reached for the best. He invited the quintet from Shinnston High School to play against his team on dedication night. The fact that Weirton was only in its first season of varsity competition, or that Shinnston was a state powerhouse, didn't bother him.

When the visitors from Shinnston took the floor for the pregame warm-up, their advantage was painfully obvious. They towered. Among the more unsettling sights was the tallest center in the state, and he was a *substitute*. Uneasiness spread among the Weirton rooters before the starting whistle. Dismay followed it.

By halftime Shinnston had whizzed to a 58–0 lead. In the second half they used their three substitutes and still the score climbed and climbed and climbed.

With six seconds remaining, a Weirton player got the ball five feet from the basket. All around him Shinnston players yelled, "Shoot! Shoot!" But he froze, and time ran out.

The next day the local newspaper, *The Clarksburg Exponent,* described the game in one paragraph below the headline:

SHINNSTON HIGH
WINS ONE-SIDED GAME
FROM WEIRTON BY BIG SCORE

That night in 1918, Shinnston had defeated Weirton (which tried four field goals and three free throws and missed them all) by the widest shutout margin in high school history—136–0.

Weirton's old gym building is still standing, and the new gym is still in use, but Weirton and Shinnston never met again on the basketball court.

Stretching the point. In 1978 the Chinese national basketball team uncovered its secret weapon, a giant player named Mu Tieh-Chu.

Chu didn't run or jump well. He didn't have to. At 7'9¾" he could dunk the ball without leaving the ground.

Called for traveling. Say a few kind words for the city of Toledo? You won't even get a kind syllable from the Colonel White High School basketball team of Dayton, Ohio.

On January 7, 1980, the 36-member traveling party took a 7-hour, 300-mile, $550 trip across the state to play Spencer-Sharples High in Toledo. They would have done better to read their horoscopes and stay in bed. All they saw was a lonely boy shooting baskets in the playground. Spencer-Sharples had been closed because of a $4.3-million cut in the Toledo public school budget.

Slip of the wrist. The Washington Bullets were leading the Indiana Pacers, 120–117 in a game on January 30, 1980. One second remained.

Pacer forward Mickey Johnson had been fouled by Bullet Bobby Dandridge in the backcourt. Johnson thus had a three-to-make-two opportunity. By missing two of them—and some luck— he could force an overtime.

Johnson hit his first shot, his fortieth point. He missed the second intentionally. On the third, he planned to bounce the ball off the rim, allowing a Pacer teammate to snare the ball and flip it in, tying the score.

Johnson stepped to the line and lofted a moon ball. *It went in.*

The Pacers went down, 120–119.

Hi, scorer. Walter Garrett wasn't a one-man team, but he was definitely a one-man offense. He scored all the points for his West End High School quintet as it walloped Glenn High, 97–54.

Walter's phenomenal performance had been mapped out before the two Birmingham (Alabama) schools met on January 11, 1963. His teammates wanted him to break the city record of 60 points in a single game, set in 1958. Their strategy: no one but Walter would shoot.

Walter connected on more than 70 percent of his floor shots and added 19 of 27 free throws. He hit from the corners, from inside, from 30 feet—from everywhere. He even put in a pair of beautiful two-handed dunk shots, something he'd never even tried in practice.

By the fourth quarter, the 6'6", 180-pound senior had amassed 74 points. Glenn High went into a stall. With six minutes left, all five Glenn players guarded him. They knew no one else would attempt a basket, and they battled to keep him from reaching the 100-point milestone.

They succeeded. His 23 fourth-quarter points over and through a beehive of arms left him three short of the magical 100. But his one-man team total of 97 points carried him into the record book.

At a loss for a win. California Institute of Technology's junior varsity basketball team lost a record 148 straight Southern California Intercollegiate Conferences before defeating LaVerne's JV, 65–61, on January 23, 1980. Tech hadn't won a conference game since 1966, when the team had been formed.

Buried within the streak was a smaller streak. Between 1972 and 1979, Tech lost 99 consecutive games against all opponents.

Foul play. In a game that saw almost as many fouls as points, Grafton downed Weston, 61–55, on New Year's Day, 1954.

The two West Virginia teams set a national high-school record with 110 fouls. Weston committed 59 and Grafton 51.

The referee's whistle took more punishment than

the gym floor, and the stop-action ended pretty much as it began. After the first three seconds, Weston scored on a foul shot. A Grafton player was at the foul line when the game ended.

Born free. Lloyd Free, 28, of the Golden State Warriors, changed his name in 1981. His new name: World B. Free.

When he was a teenager in the ghetto, he said, everybody had a nickname. A classmate gave him "World," and the label stuck.

"I'm moving up in the world," said the NBA star. "So I thought I'd better do something to commemorate it."

What if he marries and has a son?

"I'll call him Second World B. Free," said the original. "And the next one will be Third World B. Free."

Loser and still champion. High-scoring Cory Zelnik, 16, captain of the Lenox School team in New York City, was often asked if his right arm was bionic. His teammates should have been asked if theirs were glass.

During the 1980–81 season, Cory, 5'11" scored 250 points in five straight games (43, 43, 53, 51, 60)—all *losses*. In the second quarter of his 53-pointer, he broke his nose but continued to whiff the nets.

Sorry, wrong number. Athens High School in Ohio jumped to a 7–0 lead before archrival Waverly High had even touched the ball in their February 19, 1982 game.

The Waverly coach had incorrectly entered even numbers for all twelve of his players in the official scorebook. He had copied them from his roster for tournament games, in which the home team wore white jerseys and even numbers, instead of from his regular league roster, in which the team wore dark jerseys and odd numbers. The officials had no choice but to call five technical fouls—one for each of the starters' incorrect numbers—and give Athens the ball out of bounds.

Steve Bruning of Athens made all five of the free throws, and so Athens had possession of both a 5–0 lead and the ball as play began. "Woody" Mayles shot, but missed, and Mike Croci took the rebound and scored for a 7–0 lead.

It was all downhill from there. Athens won an Olympian victory, 72–49.

Wait till the sun shines, Nellie. The wettest day for basketball was February 1, 1973. Rain washed out the game between the women's teams of the University of Miami and Barry College, slated for Miami's outdoor court.

Enshrine the day. It marked the last time a college basketball game had to be called because of an all-court dunk.

Wake me when it's over. The most humiliating whitewash in girls' basketball was inflicted by Alluwe upon Chelsea in an Oklahoma high school game. Alluwe won, 106–0.

The game, if you can call it that, was played in Chelsea's new gym on January 2, 1931. Alluwe took the floor sporting black shorts and orange tops with a black A in front and numbers on the back. Chelsea wore homemade uniforms of green and white checkered rompers. The difference was more than cotton deep. Alluwe had fielded winning sextets for several years.

Chelsea was in its first season of varsity basketball.

Before the game, John Franklin, Alluwe's coach, instructed his girls to feed the ball to Juanita Reed, a 5'8" senior and the team's best shooter. The girls got the ball to Juanita as per instructions, and she scored all the field goals. Manilla Pannell, the other forward, and Juanita's closest friend, shot all the free throws.

The action itself was like instant replay. Alluwe's jump center, Hazel Tilly, batted the ball to either Juanita or Manilla, and they almost always scored or rebounded.

The baskets came so easily that the Alluwe girls lost count—till they were told that 100 points was within reach. Then they played even harder. Juanita, who stayed in the entire game, did not realize that she had scored 92 points until she was asked to pose for a newspaper photographer.

Half a century later she commented, "With all due respect to the Chelsea team, I wish all of life would have been as easy as that game."

Eva Stierwalt, who was a 5'2", 15-year-old sophomore guard for the losers, recalled the afternoon with a contrasting emotion. Her team had tried three field goals and three foul shots and missed them all. "If I'd been a crying person," she said, "I'd probably have been in tears at the end. But I wasn't. I've tried for fifty years to forget that game!"

Breaking up is hard to do. The girls' teams of East Ridge and Ooltewah High Schools in Tennessee set a record on January 7, 1969, that no one is aching to better. The East Ridge sextet wobbled to a 38–37 win after *16 overtimes.*

When the regulation game ended in a 34–34 tie, the endurance test began. It wasn't till around the tenth overtime that the teams scored again. Nobody was certain of the period.

"We played so long," said Betty Robinson, coach of Ooltewah, the home team. "I just can't remember exactly."

East Ridge's Cindy Straussburger, the game's high scorer with 19 points, sank a basket with two seconds to go. Ooltewah, it appeared, would need a miracle to tie. They got one. Debbie Goodman took the pass-in near the midline and simply flung the ball. It dropped in as the horn sounded, knotting the score at 36–36 and dooming the girls to more overtimes.

The teams couldn't add more points till five seconds were left in the sixteenth overtime. East Ridge's Straussburger hit a two-pointer. She was penalized, however, for charging after the basket. Ooltewah's Goodman stepped to the foul line for one and one, and the chance to even the score again and send the game into eternity.

Goodman sank the first shot but flubbed the second. At least it broke the monotony.

The All-American dollar sign. Center Moses Malone signed a $13-million contract in 1982 to play with the Philadelphia '76ers. That's $1 million more than it cost to build the arena where he would play, the Spectrum, in 1967.

Defeat is catching. With one second left in the game against Atlanta on January 8, 1982, Milwaukee's Harvey Catching jumped high to block a desperation shot from midcourt. He accidentally tipped it into the basket, gifting Atlanta with a 90–88 victory.

Making a point. Open the record books and you might see it buried among lesser facts. The date was February 25, 1924. The state was Maryland. The teams were Central High School of Lonaconing and Ursuline Academy of Cumberland. The score was 162–3. And finally you come to it: Marie Boyd of Central scored 77 field goals and two free throws.

Even in these days of machine-gun scoring, no individual, male or female, has come close to matching Marie's 156 points. Her performance is even more astounding because she accomplished it in a day of center jumps after every basket. The girls' game was further encumbered by the three-section court. Each team had two forwards, center and side center, and two guards, and none could leave her section. Only three dribbles were permitted.

The day before the game with Ursuline, Central's coach, Dr. Henry Hodgson, had his players working to perfect a tip-off play. The purpose was to get the ball to Marie, a tall, handsome girl and the team's high scorer.

The practice bore undreamed-of results against the shorter, outclassed Ursuline sextet. The action was a study in repetition. Central's center batted the ball to the side center, who tossed the ball to Marie under the basket. It was almost impossible to stop her from sinking lay-ups.

Even the fans who squeezed into Central's matchbox gym in 1924 scarcely believed their eyes. Later, basketball buffs dismissed the feat as impossible. After all, female sports in that era were considered little more than a necessary evil. Girls, it was held, are too emotional, and basketball is an emotional sport. How could a girl score 156 points?

Marie Boyd did, and her name is in the record books.

It's been so long. When Joe Barantovich took over as coach of the girls' team at Southwest Miami (Florida) High School in 1981, he needed his sense of humor. The Eagles hadn't won a game in three years, and the forecast was for extended disaster.

"We have the best outside shooters in the country," Barantovich quipped. "The trouble is that we play all our games indoors."

Despite Barantovich's good humor and honest effort, his girls continued to get smeared. Coral Gables thumped them, 57–28, in the next-to-last game of the season. For Southwest, the defeat was an embarrasing landmark. Not only did it raise the team's won-lost count to 0–17 for the season, but it also established a national high school record for consecutive losses, 64.

Getting smeared, however, is an acquired habit, and Southwest suddenly kicked it. On February 10, 1982, the skies cleared. After waiting 1,104 days between victories, Southwest triumphed, 48–40, over South Dade in the final game of the season.

Marshall Mishappiness. February 2, 1982, wasn't a night that Con Marshall, sports information director at Chadron (Nebraska) State College, would care to see repeated in this life or any other.

The series of misadventures began with a basketball game against Wayne State. The four officials were 45 minutes late for the tip-off. They had been stopped for speeding and fined, $112 all together.

Then the person singing the national anthem forgot the words.

Next, the star of the halftime show, a karate expert, had his problems with a stack of bricks. After four attempts, he finally hacked apart eight of them.

In what should have been the finale, Chadron State faltered in the second half and lost its seventeenth game of the season, 71–65. But it wasn't over yet.

The following day a nationally syndicated radio commentator got hold of the night's mishaps. In his noon broadcast he incorrectly named Marshall as the singer who had fumbled the national anthem.

It was an evening that had definitely started on the wrong note.

II.

Diamond
Dillies
(Baseball)

Here's mud in your eye. The Detroit Tigers of the early 1970s lacked running speed. To counteract the swiftness of opposing teams the Detroit groundkeepers watered down the base paths, especially the takeoff section by first base.

One for the road. Having retired the first two batters, pitcher Mike Lee of the Portland Beavers retired himself.

With Portland ahead of Vancouver, 8–3, in the ninth inning, Lee, a 29-year-old reliever, got the first batter on a fly ball. He struck out the second. Then he called his manager from the dugout and abruptly strode off the mound. He tossed aside his glove and cap and stripped off his uniform shirt on the way to the clubhouse.

"I chose the way I wanted to go out," Lee said after the Pacific Coast League game on August 16, 1982. He had a 0–5 record and an earned run average of 4.80 in 24 appearances for the Beavers that season. "I always wanted to strike out the last man I faced in pro ball."

Home is where the plates are. The 1981 college game between Pembroke State and North Carolina–Charlotte in North Carolina was called after 9 innings because of hunger. The score was tied, 8–8.

"It was six twenty-five and growing dark," explained Harold Ellen, the Pembroke State coach. "We have field lights, but the dining hall closes at six-thirty."

A little on the side. Reggie Jackson, a high-salaried outfielder, had a miserable year at bat for the New York Yankees in 1981. Angry fans didn't hide their frustration. They threw money. Not just nickles and dimes, but dollar bills.

What did Jackson do about the bills and coins? He picked them up. On a bad day, (or rather, a good one) he collected close to $100.

Of Corsicana. His name was Justin Clark, hardly a household word, then or now. He never was nominated for the Hall of Fame or had his full-color portrait on a baseball card. Yet for one fantastic game, he was baseball's greatest slugger.

He spent most of his 25-year career in the minor leagues. From 1905–20 he made glancing appearances in the majors with Cleveland, Detroit, and St. Louis in the American League, and with Philadelphia and Pittsburgh in the National League. In 506 games as a big leaguer, his batting average was an unheroic .254. He hit only six home runs.

In the minors he was something else—a feared left-handed power hitter. On June 15, 1902, he did what no other hitter in professional baseball has ever done, before or since.

He came to bat eight times and hit eight home runs.

On that Sunday afternoon, Clark, 19, was catching for Corsicana against Texarkana in the Texas League. The game was held at the ballpark in Ennis, where the outfield fences were close in. But take nothing away from him. By all accounts his eight homers cleared the fences with yardage to spare. Corsicana won by a score remote from civilization, 51–3.

Several newspapers of the day printed the score as 5–3. The editors believed that 51–3 had to be an error and blamed the wireless operator.

Why was this man smiling? Pitcher Tommy Boggs was paid $120,000 by the Atlanta Braves in 1981, his fifth losing season in six years. He finished with a 3–13 record that included a wretched 4.10 earned-run average. Because he always did his best and didn't complain, he demanded a raise for 1982—and got it.

Well, blow me away. During the 1961 All-Star game in San Francisco, the Giants' right-hander Stu Miller was called for a balk when a gust of wind nudged him off the mound.

Fit to be tied. Were it not for the uniforms, spectators at a baseball game between Brooklyn and Boston on August 18, 1910, couldn't have told the teams apart.

Each team scored 8 runs and had 13 hits, 5 strikeouts, 3 walks, 38 at-bats, 1 hit batter, 2 errors, 12 assists, and 1 passed ball.

Next time, tiptoe through the tulips. Texas Rangers' relief pitcher Steve Cromer injured himself walking from the bullpen to the clubhouse after a game against Toronto in 1982. He caught his right foot in a drain and broke a small bone, sidelining him for a month.

Goode for her. The strangest incident in the 1947 World Softball Championship occurred in the Washington-Fresno women's game. Dolores Goode, at bat for Washington with two outs in the fifth inning, swung and missed the third strike. The catcher dropped the ball but threw quickly to first base. The first basewoman, without touching the bag, walked off the field, and so did the rest of the Fresno team. With only the umpires for company, Goode trotted around the bases for a Washington run.

Handy man. Sam Sorce played all nine positions for the University of Miami when his team whipped St. Leo College, 14–2, on the night of April 21, 1981.

Although he considered himself a pitcher, the junior from LaGrange Park, Illinois, had been batting .365 as Miami's designated hitter. His number, 10, fit his performance in the St. Leo game. He started as the catcher and worked his way around the field—a college first.

He made putouts at four positions, and in the third inning started a double play. He pitched a scoreless ninth inning, improving his 2.67 earned-run average. In the fourth inning he hit a two-run double that broke a 2–2 tie and helped Miami to its forty-sixth victory in 51 games.

Play ball, play ball, play ball. The Pawtucket (Rhode Island) Red Sox and the Rochester (New York) Red Wings were just two ordinary teams in the International League—till they played the longest game in the history of organized baseball.

The game began at 8 P.M., April 18, 1981. Eight hours and 7 minutes later, the score was tied, 2–2, after 32 innings. It was then 4:07 the next morning—Easter Sunday—and the umpires cried, "Enough!"

For the statistically minded, there had been 156 baseballs used and 212 at-bats; 59 batters had struck out, 22 had walked, and 49 had been stranded on base.

Two months later, on June 23, the game resumed. Pawtucket won, 3–2, in the bottom of the thirty-third inning when Dave Koza lashed a bases-loaded single.

Among the truckload of records broken were two that missed official notice: staying power (both teams) and holding power (all umpires).

Bragged Jack Lietz, the chief umpire, "We went the entire game without going to the bathroom."

Hidden ball trick. When the Senators opened the 1958 season against the Red Sox, President Dwight D. Eisenhower threw out the traditional first ball with his autograph on it. All the players scampered after it— except Jimmy Piersall of the Red Sox.

The zany, high-strung Piersall was well known for his colorful antics. While the players of both teams were scrambling after the President's throw, Piersall strolled over to the box seats. He had hidden a ball in his glove, and he asked Ike to sign it.

"I never did like crowds," he said.

Half-baked. With his team leading, 8–0, Ed Myers, catcher for Fredonia (Arizona) High School, caught a pitch and threw toward third base, seemingly in an attempt to pick off runner Bill Robertson of Ash Fork High. The throw flew into left field.

Robertson raced for home with an apparent run, only to be tagged out before his foot touched the plate. Myers had the ball hidden in his catcher's mitt all the time. What he'd thrown into left field was a potato, a good "throwing potato," which he'd bought for 20 cents. While Robertson and his teammates protested, most of the evidence was eaten by Dave Jackson, Fredonia's left fielder.

The umpires huddled with the rule book but could find no grounds for objection. When the fun had gone on long enough, Fredonia coach Clint Long allowed Robertson to be called safe.

After the game, won by Fredonia, 18–7, on April 28, 1981, Coach Long explained. "If I'd let Robertson be called out," he said, "baseball players would be firing potatoes all over the place next year."

Coach Long had pulled the trick because Ash Fork's coach, Lynn Painter, a close friend, was leaving to coach baseball in Colorado.

"I thought it would be appropriate," said Long, "to give Lynn something to remember from a bunch of half-baked Arizonians."

Little pitchers have big years. Pitcher Steve Carlton of the Phils had a 27–10 record in 1972, when Philadelphia had won only 59 games. Thus Carlton, by himself, accounted for nearly half—45.7 percent—of his team's victories during the season.

All in the family. Don Nielsen broke two bones in his leg sliding into second base during a softball game in 1981. He wound up in the same hospital room at the Maine Medical Center with his wife, Rita, and their newborn daughter, Kristin Anne.

Fly ball. The bird appeared in the eighth inning, swooping lazily above the 1978 baseball game between High Point and Catawba colleges in North Carolina.

The feathered fan hovered unnoticed till a High Point batter whacked an easy fly to center field. Bird and ball collided in midair. Instead of a sure out, the ball fell for a base hit, scoring two runs and aiding High Point to a 14–10 triumph.

The bird didn't wait to be thanked. It veered off, somewhat bruised, thoroughly startled, but still flapping.

Switch pitcher. A trio of Baltimore left-handed hitters was due at bat in the fourth inning of an American Association championship game on July 18, 1882. So Tony Mullane, the Louisville pitcher, changed his delivery from right hand to left, and retired the side. Switching from left to right and back again, he eventually lost on a homer, 9–8, with two out in the ninth.

A leading pitcher in the majors in the nineteenth century, Mullane was a consistent 30-game winner. He might have been voted into Baseball's Hall of Fame, but he was suspended for the 1885 season for having signed contracts with several clubs the year before.

Time has hazed over his pen hand. He may have used both.

Winning in a walk. The Crescent High School girls' softball team of Iva, South Carolina, got only three hits against McCormick High. But Crescent wound up winning 34–5 in the first game of a doubleheader in 1981. Crescent was helped by 42 walks in the five-inning game.

Crescent also won the second game, 24–4, but had to do some running. McCormick gave up only 19 walks.

They like it like that. Forest City, of Cleveland, scored 90 runs in the first inning against a Utica team in 1870 and had the bases loaded with no one out when rain stopped play. In the same year, Forest City crunched the Brooklyn Atlantics, 132–1, in five innings.

Play it again, Sam. Baseball fans who watched Oklahoma State defeat South Carolina, 8–5, in the first round of the 1981 College World Series had to stand for the national anthem twice.

The organist played it through once, but the vocalist refused to sing with accompaniment. She finally performed a cappella.

Not a baa-ad job. A goat assisted the groundkeeper in trimming the outfield grass in Sportsman's Park, St. Louis, during the 1930s.

Wright on. Among the freakiest streaks in baseball is the American League runs-batted-in record set by Taft Wright, a White Sox outfielder.

A .300 hitter, Wright drove in at least one run in 13 straight games in 1941. The string was launched on May 4 with a single and ended May 21.

The freaky side of the record is that in 6 of the 13 games Wright went hitless. He drove in runs with walks, infield outs, and sacrifice flies.

Hurts so good. Seattle fans gaped in disbelief as Tony Conigliaro of Boston walked slowly and deliberately around the bases after slamming a third-inning home run on July 25, 1969. They didn't know he had wrenched his back from the swing and was unable to run.

Hello, good-bye. The Phillies' Tim McCarver lost a grand-slam home run (July 4, 1976) when he overtook teammate Gary Maddox on the basepath. Maddox, on first, had started for second when he decided McCarver's hit could be caught. He was doubling back to first when McCarver passed him. Fortunately for Maddox, his team won, 10–5, saving him from immortality as a goat.

Long day's journey into night. Fred Toney of Winchester in the Blue Grass League pitched 17 no-hit innings on May 10, 1909, before beating Lexington, 1–0.

41

Always leave 'em laughing. The record for the greatest number of passed balls by a major league catcher in a single game is six. The dubious honor belongs to Cincinnati's Harry P. "Rube" Vickers, who trimmed his sorry performance with comic relief. He blew his nose before strolling after the ball and smoked a cigarette in the batter's box.

A parcel of unusual conditions produced his antics. It was October 4, 1924, the closing day of the 1902 National League season. Cincinnati demanded the game be cancelled because rain had turned the field into mire. Pittsburgh's Barney Dreyfuss insisted on playing. He wanted his Pirates to break the record by winning 103 games in a single season.

Cincinnati's manager, Joe Kelly, gave in, but he showed his displeasure by presenting a comedy routine. He started Vickers, a pitcher, behind the plate. He put shortstop Tommy Corcoran on second base and staffed the rest of the infield with left-handers: Noodles Hahn at first; Cy Seymour at third; and Mike Donlin at shortstop. First baseman Jack Beckley took the mound and was relieved by Donlin and Seymour, both outfielders.

During the game the Cincinnati players puffed cigarettes on the field. Vickers, who caught a few innings only, smoked at bat. When Umpire Hank O'Day ordered him to toss the butt away, he stubbornly refused. Chief Zimmer, the Pittsburgh catcher, snatched it from his lips and hurled it to the grass.

Vickers was not cowed. Before doing his slow-step after each ball that got away from him, he paused to

blow his nose. His teammates rocked with laughter as he went into the act of carefully unfolding and folding his handkerchief.

Pittsburgh was so outraged by Cincinnati's clowning that Barney Dreyfuss threatened to bring charges against Joe Kelly for "unbecoming conduct on the field." Kelly retorted with a blast of his own: Dreyfuss should be arrested for opening the gates on such a soggy bummer of a day.

The threats were merely threats. No one was satisfied except the fans. Uncertain whether to be amused or angered by the monkeyshines, they went home happy: Pittsburgh refunded their money at the gate.

And—oh, yes. Pittsburgh won, 11–2, thus setting the record of 103 victories. It remained unbroken until 1906, when the Chicago Cubs won 116.

Catch-as-catch-can. On May 23, 1954, five Cardinals came to bat in the eighth inning against Cincinnati, but the Red's catcher, Ed Bailey, did not handle a single pitch. Red Schoendiest and Stan Musial singled on the first throw of pitcher Jackie Collum. Collum was relieved by Frank Smith, who threw only three pitches as Ray Jablonski, Tom Alston, and Rip Repulski flied out. The Reds won, 13–6.

Once in a lifetime. Pitcher Hoyt Wilhelm of the Giants hit a home run his first time at bat (April 23, 1952). Wilhelm pitched in 1,070 major league games but never homered again.

The Stark truth. When the Dodgers played in Ebbett's Field, Brooklyn, a local businessman named Abe Stark put up a sign in right field offering a free suit to any hitter striking it.

III.

Huddling, Muddling, and Befuddling (Football)

S'no fun. Hero of the 13–13 tie between Washington State College and San Jose State, played at Pullman, Washington, in 1955, was Charles Moore, 17. He ch-ch-cheered.

Charles sat in the grandstand surrounded by rows of silent, empty seats. A solitary figure, he watched the game through falling snow while the temperature hovered near zero and coffee froze in the press box. There was a smattering of 424 other hardy fans in the stadium, but all of them had purchased their tickets in advance. Charles was the one and only soul to brave the fierce weather and buy a ticket at the gate, a three-dollar seat.

He was rewarded by Washington State for his loyal support with a three-dollar refund and by reams of newspaper publicity. The attention surprised him. He really hadn't minded the cold. Golly, no. He lived in nearby Harrington, which is known in the region as "the ice box."

Losing contact. New York State Institute of Technology defeated Rensselaer Polytechnic Institute, 21–8, on October 10, 1981. Rensselaer's lone score was set up by a 63-yard pass to a receiver whose position was unexpectedly wide open.

After looking at the game films, New York's coach, Marty Senall, noticed his freshman defensive back, John Smith, standing like a statue while the Rensselaer receiver raced past him.

"Smitty, why didn't you move?" demanded the coach.

"I didn't dare," Smith answered. "My contact lens had popped out, and I was marking the spot with my foot till I had time to find it and put it back. My folks would have creamed me for losing it."

No time for glory. Most of the 85,000 fans in Yankee Stadium were on their feet and screaming in the final seconds of the 1928 Army-Notre Dame game. Army, trailing by six points, had driven to the Notre Dame one-yard line.

Notre Dame's All-American guard, George Leppig, knew Spike Nave, the Army quarterback, and thought he could influence him with a little psychological shake-up.

"Spike," he said. "Don't you wish you had another time-out?"

The trick worked. The Army quarterback thought he had used up all his time-outs and let the clock run out. Notre Dame escaped with a 16–12 victory.

Party pooper. After a record 50 defeats in a row, Macalaster College in St. Paul, Minnesota, won its 1981 opener against Wisconsin's Mt. Senario College, 17–14. Not everyone welcomed the victory, however.

"We party before and after every home loss," a sophomore lamented. "Now there won't be anything to look forward to."

Water, water everwhere. A college game produced a total of *minus* 5 yards rushing.

Wisconsin-Stevens Point defeated Wisconsin-Superior, 35–27, during a downpour that erased the field and threatened to drown the running backs. Stevens Point sloshed for 11 yards on the ground. Superior skidded and slid for minus 16.

The only way linemen could stand was to hang onto someone else, and they took turns pulling each other down. As a result, 24 penalties totaling 265 yards were called.

Some 350 spectators watched the contest on October 17, 1981. They knew it was football and not mud-wrestling because they frequently spied a ball in the air. The two teams attempted 135 passes and completed 72 for 953 yards.

The swampfest lasted 3 hours and 55 minutes and waterlogged 9 footballs.

Hamstrung. There's an old saying about things going wrong. . . .

The 1982 Baltimore Colts were floundering through a miserable, hard-luck 2–14 season when they squared

off against the St. Louis Cardinals on November 22. Robert Pratt, the Colt's offensive guard and a team captain, was summoned to midfield for the coin toss.

Pratt strained a hamstring muscle trotting out!

The injury forced him from the game early and sidelined him the following Sunday, snapping his 104-game playing streak, the longest on the club.

Naturally, the Colts lost the coin toss—and the game.

Where there is a will. The smallest college football player ever was Billy Barty, who played five quarters for Los Angeles City College in 1945. Barty stood 3'9" and weighed 86 pounds.

A 21-year-old senior, he was used as a flanker and halfback. Seven plays (and two uniforms) were designed especially for him. Four plays used him as a decoy, and in the others he threw a pass, caught a lateral, or ran out as a receiver.

Barty never let his size handicap him. He ran 50 yards in 7.2 seconds, 100 yards in 14.5 seconds, high-jumped 4'2", and broad-jumped 13'9".

He was also the shortest college basketball player, earning a letter on the first basketball team to represent Los Angeles State College. Later he joined the alumni quintet for games against the Athletic Department. He once scored 16 points while guarding Hall-of-Famer Bill Sharman.

"Billy," complained Sharman. "Get away from my knees!"

Monday mourning cornerback. Terrance Smith, 27, of Richland, Washington, contributed the screwball play of the 1970 college season. He entered the game between Washington State and Stanford as a volunteer.

The ball was on Washington State's 25-yard line. Eric Cross of Stanford took a handoff and sprinted to his left. As he turned the corner, Smith, a loyal Washington fan, dashed from the stands. He put a vicious but unavailing tackle on Cross at the two-yard line. Cross's second effort carried him in for the touchdown.

Smith's heroics wouldn't have altered the outcome, even if he'd stopped Cross. Washington got walloped, 63–16.

Bald is beautiful. Fritz Von Berg followed a dream. He tried out for the football team at Monterey Peninsula Junior College in 1980. He stood 5'10" and weighed a solid 180 pounds, but none of the other players wanted to hit him. It would be like hitting Daddy.

Von Berg was bald, bearded, and *49 years old.*

Still, he made the team as defensive middle guard, by far the oldest player in National Collegiate Athletic history. He missed only two games in two seasons for the Lobos, a California power in Division II. He pulled a calf muscle.

A journalism major, Von Berg had been working since he was nine, and he'd had to postpone a lot of his ambitions. One was to play football.

"The time was never right before this, but I've got a rule about life," he said. "Better late than never."

Ladies Day. C. W. Staley of Vinton, Iowa, invented a means to allow women to play on men's football teams and score like superstars.

In 1977, Staley, a retired Baptist minister, took out the first of his patents on "CHEEReceiver." The invention consisted of a giant, football-shaped metal frame designed to stand behind each goalpost. A cheerleader perched upon the frame and doubled as a receiver.

This "equal opportunity specialist," as Staley termed her, would attempt to catch the ball on conversions and field goals. If she succeeded, her team would be awarded four extra points. When not involved in the play, she would entertain the crowd. Staley maintained that she would make end-zone seats as popular as those on the 50-yard line.

CHEEReceiver didn't exactly raise tidal waves of enthusiasm in the National Football League. But Staley did get sprayed with attention for using the abbreviation of his company's name, National Football Ladies, Inc. That's NFL.

Running to nowhere. The woeful New England Patriots and the equally woeful Baltimore Colts closed the 1981 season against each other. At stake was the title, "Worst Team in the NFL."

The first six plays from scrimmage illustrated how deserving both teams were. In order, the plays went: 1) Patriot Vegas Ferguson was dumped for a one-yard loss; 2) After New England was penalized five yards for a false start, Sam Cunningham galloped for no gain; 3)

Quarterback Tom Owen was sacked; he fumbled but recovered for an eight-yard loss; 4) Rich Camarillo punted to Colt Ray Butler, who fumbled and the Patriots recovered—but the play was called back because of a Patriot penalty; 5) Punting again, Camarillo butter-fingered the snap and boomed an eight-yarder. 6) Colt Curtis Dickey was smeared for a two-yard loss.

Thereafter, ardor cooled and plays were run with surprising mediocrity. The Colts stumbled to a 23–21 win, leaving both teams with a 2–14 record and the title of "worst" team hanging in air.

Having an ice time, wish you were here—in my place. Under conditions ideal for curling up in an igloo with a good book, the Cincinnati Bengals met the San Diego Chargers on January 10, 1982. The vital statistics weren't turnovers or time of possession, but thermometer degrees. It was *cold.*

The temperature had dropped to nine degrees below zero at game time. Icy winds gusted up to 35 mph. The wind-chill factor, misery's carrier, hit a hair-stiffening 59 below.

A crowd of 46,302 proved their loyalty, if not their intelligence, by sitting outdoors in Cincinnati's Riverfront Stadium. Another 13,277 ticketholders displayed their devotion to health and welfare by staying at home.

"I wouldn't send my dog out in this weather," said Kellen Winslow, the Chargers' all-pro tight end.

Anthony Munoz, the Bengals' tackle, stubbornly

held to his habit of playing bare-armed. "I didn't realize they were numb because my face hurt so much," he said.

Bengals quarterback Kenny Anderson suffered frostbite of the right ear. Chargers' quarterback Dan Fouts departed the field with icicles glistening in his beard.

It was so cold that pipes froze in the rest rooms. A fleet of heated city buses was kept outside the stadium with a supply of blankets borrowed from local hospitals. Police climbed the stands in search of anyone who needed emergency aid.

Not to be forgotten, the Bengals drew with the elements and beat the Chargers, 27–7, to win the AFC championship and the right to go to the Super Bowl.

When a prune is a lemon. Northeastern State University of Tahlequah, Oklahoma, was searching for a new mascot in 1981. The caricature of an Indian had fallen into disfavor.

A woman dressed as a prune showed up at the homecoming game on October 17.

"I received strange looks from the cheerleaders, and the athletes were definitely unfriendly," she said. She asked not to be identified. "I don't want to be firebombed in the middle of the night."

Clearly, a giant prune was not the answer—but it did add a new wrinkle to the search.

If at first you don't succeed. Jack Mackmull made all the extra points in Army's 35–0 battering of Fordham on November 5, 1949. The second conversion required

real kick-to-itiveness. He had to boot the ball five times.

His first attempt was good, but it was cancelled as Army was penalized 15 yards. His second attempt was also good, but it was nullified by another 15-yard penalty. He missed his third and fourth tries, but Fordham was offside both times. His fifth sailed between the uprights, and as neither Army nor Fordham was flagged for an infraction, it counted.

Don't give up the ship. Coach Don Ruggeri of the Massachusetts Maritime Academy started the 1980 football season with the most inexperienced eleven in the country. Forty-two of his players were aboard ship on a 60-day cruise off the east coast. That left him with a makeshift squad of six seniors and 32 freshmen.

The cruise was supposed to have been completed before the first game. Mechanical problems caused delays, and the experienced players didn't return until the sixth game.

Better they had stayed on the ocean. The team went 4–1 without them and 1–2 with them.

Never say quit. The University of Wisconsin-Platteville fumbled the first four times it had the football. Each time Wisconsin-Eau Claire recovered and scored. With seven minutes left in the second quarter, the Platteville Pioneers seemed hopelessly behind, 33–0.

Nevertheless, the greatest comeback in NCAA football was about to take place. Platteville finally scored, and with seven seconds remaining in the half, scored again on 75-yard run-back of an interception. The teams went into the lockers with Platteville behind, 33–14.

In the third quarter, Platteville closed the gap to 36–22. The Pioneers were still trailing with only 12 minutes left, 43–22. They reached deep for something extra and found it. A 55-yard touchdown pass. A five-yard touchdown pass. A 45-yard punt return touchdown.

Suddenly, miraculously, the score was tied, 43–43!

Many in the Parents' Day crowd of 4,000 at Platteville on that afternoon of November 8, 1980, had already departed. Pell-mell, they hurried back into the stands.

With six minutes remaining, Platteville blocked a punt. The ball bounced through the end zone for a safety, and Platteville *led*, 45–43!

Platteville had scored 30 unanswered points in the last 12 minutes to win.

The hero among heroes? Ron Bukjo.

Ron who?

Ron Bukjo. Write his name large on the scroll of men who never give up.

Bukjo, a specialty team member, had blocked the punt that gave Platteville the lead. A senior, he didn't even travel with the squad, and he had played barely 30 seconds in his entire varsity career.

Haven can't wait. Some 400 fans turned out to watch Haven (Kansas) High School's undefeated football team play lightly regarded Sylvia High on November 16, 1927. They expected plenty of scoring, and they got it.

Haven ran nonstop through, around, and over Sylvia. When all the touchdowns were counted and recounted, checked and double-checked, Haven had won, 256–0.

Haven romped for 38 touchdowns—20 in the first half and 18 in the second (when the reserves took over) —and kicked 28 extra points. Nothing but the final whistle stopped them.

All 22 boys on the black-and-gold Haven squad were given a chance to carry the ball. Only two starters, center Charles Bachly and guard Lloyd Harris, failed to score.

Elven McCoy, a 155-pound halfback and star passer, saved his arm but didn't spare his legs. He ran for 15 touchdowns (90 points), including a 100-yarder. Jessie Atkinson, captain and quarterback, and Lloyd Shrock, substitute end, each scored 60 points. None of the three played more than a half.

Sylvia, a small school, had 70 students compared to Haven's 124, and its team was lighter and less experienced. The offense consisted mainly of punting and fumbling. The defense brought almost no one down.

Toward the end of the second quarter, spectators with weak recall had to guess at the score. The Haven scoreboard didn't register beyond 99.

The lone official, J. Burch Stuart, was too busy with his addition to bother about statistics. So was the student scorekeeper. Yards gained, distance of punts, fumbles, etc., were ignored in the race to keep up with the four-points-a-minute stampede.

Haven finished the year with a perfect 8–0 record and laid claim to the unofficial state championship. The team had outscored its opponents 579–0. Nearly half the total came against Sylvia.

Fifty-five years later the details and the emotions had faded. Few who witnessed the game recalled more than the score, 256–0. One who did remember was Alfred Collmann, and his memory included the worthiest feature of that darkly comic afternoon.

Collmann had been Haven's student athletic manager. He had stood on the sideline during the most one-sided football game in history as Haven nearly buried Sylvia in the proud wheat country of Kansas.

"Sylvia," he remembered, "fought hard."

One toe over the line. Substitute Ray Strong of the Atlanta Falcons enthusiastically cheered a teammate's interception against San Francisco in 1981—too enthusiastically. He stepped accidentally onto the field and bumped into an official. The penalty levied against the Falcons for having too many men on the field nullified the 55-yard runback.

Hold that line. A rain storm during the Wake Forest-Maryland game on October 18, 1981, knocked out telephone service. Coaches were forced to communicate between the field and the press box by walkie-talkies.

In the press box Assistant Maryland Coach Jerry Eisman was talking to his bench when a voice broke in.

"Get off," the voice ordered. "This is a police emergency frequency."

"This *is* an emergency," Eisman retorted. "It's third down!"

He couldn't bear it. James Tulley of Rockford, Illinois was so annoyed by the miserable performances of the Chicago Bears that in 1981 he sued them for passing themselves off as a professional football team. He charged false advertising and fraud.

The 31-year-old school supply salesman asked $58.40 in refunds for expenses—tickets, gas, baby-sitter, and tolls—he had laid out to see the Bears lose to the Washington Redskins.

"I went to see a professional game," he said.

Tully insisted that the loved the Bears. He just hated watching them lose and lose and lose.

"We've been rebuilding for forty-seven years," he said.

Ready, willing, and able. One of the most unusual traditions in football—a sight that puzzles newcomers—can be seen at Texas A&M. The entire cadet corps stands throughout every home game in honor of the "12th man."

The original "12th man" was a student, E. King Gill. He was helping out as a spotter in the press box when Texas A&M faced Centre College in the Dixie Classic, a postseason game in Dallas in 1922. Gill had played on the football team, but being more valuable as a basketball player, he had switched sports with the season.

Near the end of the first half he was called down to the A&M bench. Injuries had riddled the squad. Coach Dana X. Bible told him to suit up and be ready to play in an emergency.

There were no dressing rooms at the stadium. Gill and an injured player had to swap garb under the stands. Wearing the borrowed uniform, Gill reported to the bench, ready to play.

Although he was never sent in, it is his spirit, the spirit of the "12th man"—the willingness to play if needed—that the cadets personify by standing during games.

Too much too soon. Dave Smith, a wide receiver for the Pittsburgh Steelers, caught a pass and ran into the end zone in 1971. The play covered 60 yards.

It should have covered 65.

The gleeful Smith had spiked the ball before he crossed the goal line. The ball hit on the five-yard line, rolled into the end zone, and was ruled a touchback. The Chiefs took over on their 20 and eventually won, 38–16.

The goof cost the Steelers a touchdown. Had the game been close, it might have cost Smith his neck.

Mean is keen. If you're meaner than your classmates, there's a place for you in life, according to a 1981 study in Texas. It's playing linebacker on a college team.

Before you decide on a gridiron career, however, know that the same study indicates that football players, regardless of position, are more superstitious, submissive, and suspicious than nonplayers.

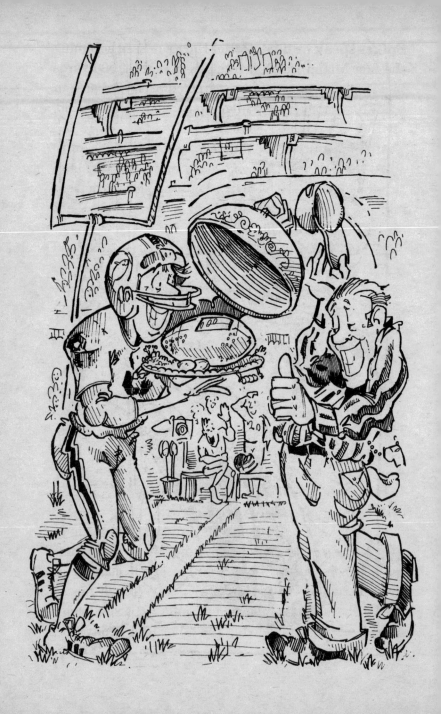

Spikes speak or bust. Duriel Harris missed becoming the first Miami Dolphin receiver to reach 1,000 yards in a single season when he scored on a 17-yard pass in a 13–10 victory over Philadelphia on November 30, 1981.

After his touchdown, Harris leaped high in the air to spike the ball, landed awkwardly on his left leg, and sprained his knee. The injury kept him out of the next game, and he played only briefly in the last two—not enough to reach 1,000 yards.

"From now on I'll just look for the referee and hand him the ball," he vowed. "My father always told me the best thing you can do is just give the ref the ball. He said that makes it seem like you've been in there a thousand times."

Springs isn't here. Tony Dorsett of the Dallas Cowboys spurted through the middle of the Minnesota Viking line for an NFL record 99-yard touchdown run in the last game of the 1982 season. He did it the hard way.

The Cowboys had only 10 men on the field. And Dorsett wasn't supposed to carry the ball.

The handoff was intended for fullback Ron Springs, who misheard the call in the huddle. The Metrodome crowd was roaring so loudly that Springs thought quarterback Danny White said "Jayhawk," which meant the Cowboys should have had a single setback. Springs dashed off the field, leaving the other back, Tony Dorsett, to grab the football and do his best with the broken play. Dorsett went 99 yards for a touchdown.

Said backfield coach Al Lavan, "I guess that play will become part of our offense now."

Band-Aided. The 1982 meeting between California and Stanford produced the wildest-ever finish in college football. A California ballcarrier snared the last of five do-or-die laterals and quick-stepped through the Stanford marching band to score the winning touchdown after time had run out.

Stanford's Mark Harmon had kicked a 35-yard field goal with four seconds remaining to give his team a 20–19 lead and, seemingly, victory. His over-enthusiastic teammates, however, charged from the sideline, believing the game was over. It wasn't. Stanford drew an unsportsmanlike conduct penalty for delay of game. Harmon had to kick off from his 25-yard line.

Before he did, California's special teams captain, Richard Rodgers, told his teammates to keep lateraling the ball if they were about to be tackled. Never was advice better heeded.

Kevin Moen fielded Stanford's short kickoff at his 45. He crossed midfield and lateraled to Rodgers, who cut toward the center of the field and flipped to Dwight Garner at the Stanford 44. Garner was driven back several yards before heaving a desperate 10-yard lateral to his right as he was being tackled.

The Stanford players on the sideline thought Garner's knee had touched the ground before he had released the ball. Again they rushed onto the field,

convinced that the game was over. They were joined by members of the Stanford band and a few cheerleaders and fans.

But no whistle had blown. The ball was not dead. The game was not over.

Rodgers caught Garner's lateral and, handling the ball for the second time, carried it into Stanford territory, where he lateraled to Mariet Ford, who raced to the Stanford 25. As two Stanford defenders closed in, Ford flung the ball blindly over his shoulder.

Moen, who had started the frantic series of laterals, snagged Ford's backward toss at the 30 and dodged through the mob of bandsmen on the field celebrating Stanford's "victory." They unwittingly provided interference for him, and he sprinted across the goal line, weaving the last yards untouched till he bowled over a Stanford trombone player in the end zone.

Final score: California, 25, Stanford, 20.

Don't blame the stork. The Huntington Locomotives steamrolled and the Long Creek Mountaineers couldn't climb onto the scoreboard in an eight-man high school game in Oregon in 1979.

The Huntington coach, Jerry Peacock, had trouble keeping the score down to 99–0. He couldn't send in a complete team of substitutes because there were but 12 boys on his squad. Even so, Huntington outmanned its opposition.

Long Creek had no substitutes at all.

Turn left at the goalpost. When Nebraska University rooters filled Memorial Stadium to watch the Cornhuskers' home games in 1981, the stadium became the third largest city in the state.

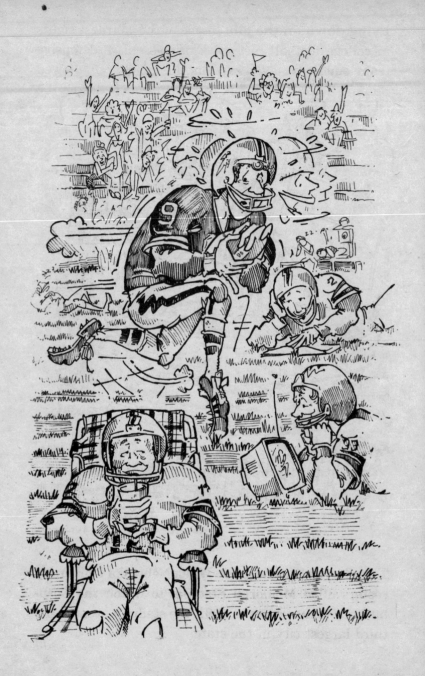

Lying down on the job. In one of the weirdest sights in college football history, Florida's entire defensive team suddenly lay down on the field and allowed Miami's John Hornibrook to score untouched from the eight-yard line.

The mass floperoo occurred with 1:10 left in the game and astounded 37,710 fans in the Orange Bowl on November 27, 1971. It was staged so that Florida's quarterback, John Reaves, a senior playing his last college game, could get his hands on the football again and have a final shot at breaking a major college passing record.

Following Miami's two-point conversion and kickoff, Reaves rushed onto the field. After throwing a near-interception, he fired a 15-yard pass to an end. The completion raised his career passing yardage to 7,546, two more than produced by Jim Plunkett of Stanford. A few seconds later, Reaves threw a three-yarder, bringing his total to 7,549.

Reaves had his record, Florida had the victory (45–16), and Florida's coach, Doug Dickey, had a kind of fame he seemed happy to live with. During a time-out, Dickey had approved the idea of letting Miami score. He stood by his decision at postgame interviews.

A seething Fran Curci, Miami's coach, called the floperoo "disgraceful" and "the worst thing I have ever seen in football."

Asked his reaction to Curci's comments, Dickey replied, "No comment. . . my responsibility is to my team, my administration, and our fans."

And so Dickey and his assistants went off to high schools to recruit football stars. Glibly they pointed out the lifetime lessons and values to be learned at the University of Florida.

Sportsmanship, unfortunately, was not among them.

Boy, did he get a wrong number. Football is a game of inches. St. Louis Cardinal punter Carl Birdsong had a clause in his 1982 contract that awarded him a $5,000 bonus if he averaged 44 yards in the regular season. He averaged 43.8. He'd have gotten the bonus if each of his 54 kicks had been just 7.2 inches longer.

IV.

Fabulous Fistivities (Boxing)

The gentle sex. A bearded pugilist named Hank Tompkins fought regularly in barroom halls in and around Pittsburgh during the late 1860s. His strapping wife disapproved of such carryings-on and let her objections be known. So before each bout he posted a burly guard outside the door to discourage interference.

On May 9, 1869, Tompkins fought Billy Franks for the championship of Pittsburgh. From the start, Tompkins took a beating. He was saved from a knockout when the bout was brought to a surprising conclusion in the sixth round. Mrs. Tompkins swept into the hall.

She had gained admittance by swatting out the guard with the best short right exhibited that afternoon. Striding between the two sweating fighters, she lifted her husband by the waist and tucked him across

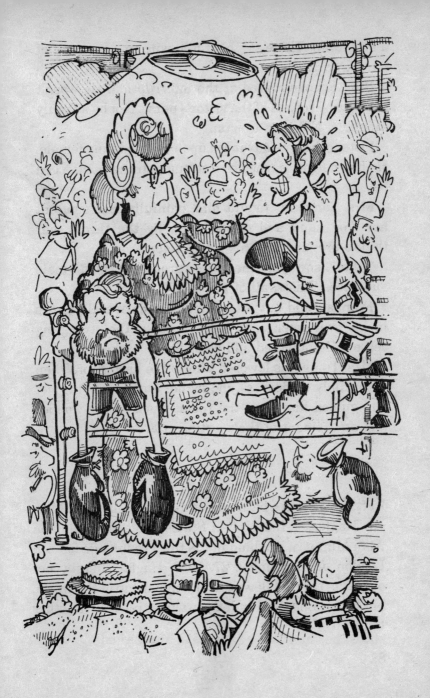

a broad hip. There she held him with one arm, out of harm's way.

Billy Franks roared at the interruption. He wasn't about to be robbed of the victor's purse. Not by a family squabble. Not by a *woman*.

Fists cocked, he advanced upon the meddling female. He had not yet learned how strong a strong woman can be.

Mrs. Tompkins taught him, painfully. She shot out her free hand and clasped him by the throat, her thumb pressing into his Adam's apple.

"Idiot!" she spat. She peered around at the all-male audience. "Idiots, all of you!"

Franks could but utter a croak and several gurgles in his own defense. In a few seconds the struggling ceased. He quivered and went limp.

Mrs. Tompkins lowered him to the hard floor. Then with wifely tenderness, she set her husband on his feet and guided him from the room, much to the wonder and amusement of the sporting crowd.

Left is right. In a battle of southpaws, challenger Marvin Hagler of the United States defeated champion Alan Minter of England in the third round of a fight in London on September 27, 1980. Hagler thereby not only won the middleweight championship of the world, but he became the first lefty to win a title from another lefty.

Hitting the headlines. For two rounds Barolo Soni and Henry Wallitsch, a pair of heavyweights, brawled evenly in Hempstead, New York, on September 12, 1959. In the third round, Wallitsch knocked himself out.

He started his trip to dreamland by throwing a right-hand haymaker and missing. The momentum carried him under the bottom strand of ropes. Leading with his chin, he hit the reporters' table and was out for five minutes.

Sweet dreams. For those who like a man of contrasts, Thomas Hearns is a good example. In 1980 Hearns won the WBA welterweight boxing title. That same year the public learned he liked to sleep with a teddy bear.

"He's got two of them, but we're always having to buy new ones because he loses them," said his manager.

Delayed action. Lightweight champion Benny Leonard hit Phil Bloom on the chin so hard during a fight in 1917 that he broke Bloom's ankle. Bloom sat on it as he went down and had to retire from the contest.

Wha'd he say? "Slapsie" Maxie Rosenbloom was a fun-loving New Yorker who punched like a kitten and talked like a paper-shredder. He held the light heavyweight title from 1930 to 1934. In 289 fights he scored a mere 18 knockouts, but in his daily bouts with pronunciation and grammar he absolutely "moidered" the English language.

Movie producers liked his comic way of speaking and cast him in character roles. He went to see his first picture, *A King for a Knight.* It was so bad that he walked out in the middle of it. Complained Maxie, "I couldn't unnerstan myself."

Knuckle down. The chap who named the tiny town of Skullbone must have been a chip off the old block, or the victim of too many good clunks on the noggin.

Skullbone got its name through fighting. The western Tennessee town was the site of bare-knuckle prizefights when the sport was illegal in most parts of the country.

The bouts were governed by an odd set of rules that required battlers to hit opponents around the head only. A punch below the collarbone was considered a foul.

Winning in a rump. Sam Langford was a short, powerful prizefighter who never weighed more than 176 pounds. Yet his savage punching terrorized heavyweights.

In 1911 Langford fought huge Jim Smith at the Atlantic Gardens in New York City. Smith was out of shape and unhappy about the match. As he passed Langford's dressing room on the way to the ring, he poked his head in and pleaded, "You gonna let me off easy, Sam, ain't you?"

"You're gonna stay so long as I think it's good for you," returned Langford.

At the bell, Smith danced madly around the ring, never giving Langford a chance to land cleanly.

In the fifth round Langford stopping chasing. He stood still and looked disgustedly at his foe. "Come on and do some fightin'," he growled.

Smith merely laughed nervously and resumed his flight.

A few seconds later Smith spun to get out of a corner. Langford seized the moment. He leaped, and with perfect timing brought a right up from his shoelaces. The punch landed flush—on the seat of Smith's pants. The towering fighter was lifted off his feet and landed on the canvas with a boom. He remained facedown, not daring to move, till the referee had tolled 10.

When at last Smith figured it was safe to stand up, he stared reproachfully at Langford and grumped, "Why you hit me there?"

"Because," Langford replied, "you got eyes in your head, but there's none you got behind you."

Bite to the finish. Two Englishmen, Arthur Chambers and Billy Edwards, fought for the lightweight crown on September 4, 1872, on Squirrel Island, Canada. At the start of the twenty-sixth round, Chambers, who had been taking a pounding, fell into a clinch. All at once he jumped back, hollering that he'd been *bitten*. Billy Tracy, the referee, saw the teeth marks and declared Chambers the winner on a foul.

The teeth marks were actually made by Tom Allen, one of Chambers's seconds, who took a bite of his battered battler between rounds and instructed him to claim a foul.

Come blow your horn. The Manhattan Opera House in New York City was the site in 1916 of a heavyweight bout that ended on a bottom note.

Halfway through the second round, Charley Weinert buckled Andre Anderson with a left hook and followed it with a looping right to the jaw. Anderson staggered backward, pitched through the ropes, and dropped into the orchestra pit amid a stack of musical instruments. He came to rest seat-first in the wide mouth of a tuba.

While the spectators howled, Anderson strove to wiggle free, but he was wedged fast. Referee Billy Joh leaned through the ropes and counted him out.

Baby strainer. Heavyweight champion Rocky Marciano threw out his back while tossing his baby daughter, Mary Ann, in the air. Doctors told him that if he continued his fighting career he might never walk properly again.

So the first-ever undefeated heavyweight champion quit the ring, victim of a nursery knockout.

Looking for work tomorrow. Junior Middleweight Champion Freddie Little defeated Gerhard Piaskowsky by a decision in 15 rounds on March 20, 1970, in Berlin, Germany. One of the judges was obviously a man of caution. He scored *every round even!*

A robe of many *phfews*. Billy Petrolle, a respected lightweight from 1924 to 1934, always entered the ring with the same old Indian blanket draped over his shoulders. The blanket had been in his family for a couple of generations, and he believed it brought him luck.

Petrolle's handlers probably wished he would wear a charm instead. They practically keeled over when he entered the ring. *The blanket had never been washed.*

Petrolle was afraid that the magic properties attached to the robe would go down the drain with the suds.

V.

Razzle-Dazzle
Roundup
(Other Sports)

Just horsing around. What's wrong with being the worst? Super Kris, a pacer, never seemed to mind. For six years he didn't win a race in 94 starts. Throw in qualifying heats, and his streak extended to 135. He ran as if limbering up for a snooze.

The United States Trotting Association was cautious about naming him the worst horse since 1803, when standard breeding had been organized. His breeder flatly refused to be interviewed. Racing fans, however, aired their opinions freely. Super Kris was definitely the crummiest.

Discovering new ways to lose was the bay gelding's hobby. Once he quit after just 25 feet, a cosmic record for a half-mile track. He lost two just-for-fun races to Beasley Reece, a speedy New York Giant defensive back, over 100 and 165 yards.

Owner-trainer-driver Tom Parcase, Jr., of Greenwood Lake, New York, brought in several veterinarians to locate Super Kris's secret. They shrugged and declared him the healthiest hopeless case they'd ever seen.

"The only way I can get a vet is to promise not to tell anyone he worked on the horse," Parcase confessed.

But you can't keep a bad horse down forever. On November 12, 1981, at Pocono Downs, Super Kris, now eight years old, went after his ninety-fifth consecutive defeat. He forgot himself and won.

The next day incredulous horse fanciers opened their newspapers and saw the picture of the finish. They thought it was trick photography.

Advice on the volley. Famed British tennis star Fred Perry was a 21-year-old rookie in 1930 on his first international tennis tour when he found himself jailed by revolutionaries in São Paulo, Brazil. The British government feared for his life.

Fortunately, Perry was recognized by a local official and allowed to complete his tour. The Brazilian added a bit of advice: "If you should be on the street and a man points a gun at you, don't panic; he won't be able to hit you. If, however, he is aiming at someone else, duck!"

Hit and run. Steve Scott combined accuracy and speed as the American mile record-holder to shoot 18 holes of golf in 29 minutes and 33.05 seconds. His time sliced 16 seconds (and 5 strokes) off the old world record.

The round was played over the H. G. "Dad" Miller Golf Course in Anaheim, California, at dawn on December 6, 1981, to raise funds for the Anaheim Parks and Recreation Department. Scott carried only one club, a 3 iron. He never went out of bounds and didn't hit a sand trap. And he scored pretty well, too. He shot a 92.

This nearly was mine. Bernie Hermsen realized every golfer's dream in 1982 at the Fox Valley Golf Club in Kaukauna, Wisconsin. He shot a hole in one.

Maybe. He'll never be sure.

Hermsen and his playing partner, Elmer Hoffman, hit tee shots into the setting sun on the 187-yard par-3 twelfth hole. No one in their foursome could follow the flight of the balls to the ground.

Walking toward the green, Hoffman spied what he thought was his ball about 15 feet from the flag. A few minutes later the other ball was found—in the hole. Hoffman and Hermsen discovered they had been using the same brand of ball. There was no way either man could identify his.

Hermsen was credited with the ace. "Somebody had to take it," he said. "They figured it was my ball because Doc [Hoffman] had claimed the first one he saw, but I have my doubts. We both want to dream that we did it."

The ultimate clogger. Henrick Doornekamp, 57, a Dutch farmer, ran in the 1980 New York City marathon wearing wooden shoes.

Marrython. The Orange Bowl Marathon in Miami, Florida, began the decade of the 1980s as a proving ground for courage, pain, and matrimony. In 1980 Ken Gomberg proposed to Debra Faillace at the 25-mile mark. The next year Bob Godwin, who couldn't wait so long, popped the question to Ann Conlin after 18 miles. Both women accepted, and both couples trotted happily across the finish line holding hands.

A capital idea. When Edward Payson Weston of Providence, Rhode Island, vowed to walk the 478 miles from Boston to Washington, D.C., he meant *every* step.

Weston started from the State House at 1 P.M. on February 22, 1861. He reached the Capitol at 5 P.M. on March 4. He had kept his word.

During a stopover in Philadelphia, a bellhop in the Continental Hotel had sought to usher him into the new steam elevator. Weston scornfully declined.

"I shall not alter my means of travel," he proclaimed, and used the stairs.

It's Greek to me. The University of Texas-El Paso won its third straight NCAA Track and Field Championship in 1981 without American aid. The team's 70 points were all scored by foreign students.

You'll get a charge out of this. For a time it looked like the outbreak of a new illness—Cheerleaders' Disease.

At Tamalpais High School in Mill Valley, California, 13 girls suffered burning eyes, itchy skin, and "tasted lemons" while practicing for a basketball halftime routine in the student center in 1982.

What's worse, their panty hose began to fall apart.

The mystery was solved when health officials sent the girls' clothing to a laboratory. The cause of the disease was not a bug, but a battery.

One cheerleader had put her pompon in the back of a station wagon, where it touched a leaky battery, absorbing acid. The acid sprayed hither and yon when she went into dance steps. All the girls recovered.

Parting is such sweet sorrow. Once there was a man in Pakistan named Islahuddin. As captain of the national field hockey team he was such a favorite that he was known by just the one name.

In 1982 Islahuddin retired after a brilliant field hockey career. His countrymen held a farewell game for him in Karachi and took up a collection among the fans in the stadium. The idea was to raise enough money to buy him a nice little going-away present. The fans poured in $2.5 million.

The amount was the highest ever given to a retiring player from Pakistan where—need it be added?—field hockey is *popular*.

A smashing start. Mayor Joseph Alioto of San Francisco tossed up the first domino at the 1970 World Domino Tournament in the Commercial Club—and broke the chandelier.

Gulls will be gulls. After a sea gull had moved pro golfer Cathy Sherk's ball during the 1982 Elizabeth Arden tournament, an official ruled that she would not be penalized two strokes because she did not see it happen.

Sherk figured she'd been penalized enough. The sea gull had picked the ball from the fairway and dropped it in the rough, leaving her a foul lie. The birdie gave her a bogie.

Can you handle this? John Gruberg, 33, invented toothbrushes mounted on tennis rackets and golf-club handles in 1981. The Fresno, California, tennis pro said that users get to practice in performing wrist actions necessary to the two games while polishing their uppers and lowers.

The brushes are ideal, Gruberg said, for any player "who can't get in a game after every meal."

That's the way the ball bounces . . . sometimes. With the score tied at 1–1, goaltender Jim Brown of the Washington Diplomats soccer team got off a punt that sailed nearly the length of the field. It took a high bounce over the head of the opposing goaltender and went into the net.

The 100-yard score enabled Washington to defeat Atlanta, 3–2, on April 5, 1981. It also marked the first time in the life of the North American Soccer League that a goaltender had made a goal.

Time out of mind. Films of the 100-meter freestyle final at the 1960 Olympics appeared to show America's Lance Larson touching ahead of Australia's John Devitt at the finish. Larson was timed at 55.1, Devitt at 55.2.

The first-place and second-place judges disagreed over who touched first, however. So the head judge stepped in and ruled in favor of Devitt, over the American team's protests. Larson's time was changed to 55.2 so that he wouldn't have a faster time than the "winner."

How funski. The Miami Ski Club, the largest ski club in America, is located in warm and sunny southern Florida, where it doesn't snow.

Lunch break. Arnold Palmer, the American golfer, was in China in 1981 to look over possible locations for a golf course. The Chinese, he discovered, knew "nothing about golf, absolutely nothing." Palmer handed a laborer a golf ball, and the man grinned and raised it toward his mouth. He wanted to take a bite out of it.

Add a dash of soy sauce, and it could be delicious.

I knew you'd blow it. Most people don't know that the bugle signal that calls horses to the post is a pantomime at most thoroughbred racetracks. Sure, the herald raises the bugle to his lips and puffs out his cheeks. But the sound heard in the stands comes from a tape.

Denise Perego, a bugler at Centennial track in Denver, wanted no part of such deception. She announced that she intended to play for real.

"I heard about the girl who worked before me," Denise said. "She dropped her bugle while the tape was going. It was so embarrassing that she quit."

Second thoughts. The ballyhoo could be heard in two countries. Jack Walsh, 31, a Hollywood stuntman, shocked the world by announcing that he was going to fight a bull with his bare hands in Tijuana, Mexico.

"Once I get him down, he's mine," Walsh proclaimed. "If I can't break his neck, I'll try karate."

On Sunday, October 16, 1961, a crowd of 6,000 crammed into the Plaza Monumental. There was the crowd and there was the bull. Only Walsh was missing. He never showed up.

Well, twist my wrist. Whenever a sports superstar signs a contract for a super sum, the average person grows hoarse gasping at such plenty. After the season, a handful of math-minded fans coldly begin dividing.

How much, say, has the Yankees' outfielder been paid per homer? The Cowboys' wide receiver per touchdown? The heavyweight champ per round?

Overlooked in the tallying is Cleve Dean, a super-heavyweight wrist-wrestling immortal. In 1978 the 6'6", 470-pound Georgia pig farmer earned $22,000 by felling the wrist of Vergil Arviero in Las Vegas. The match lated 10 seconds.

That's $132,000 per minute.

Putter there. During the 1982 U.S. Women's Open Championship, pro golfer Carolyn Hill, 23, stopped to quench her thirst. When she got to the green and reached for her putter, she remembered she had left it propped against the water cooler. Her caddie raced back for the club. Rather than delay play, the resourceful Hill pulled out her driver and sank a five-foot putt, her only birdie of the round.

Stepping up to the next tee to hit her drive, she said to her caddie, "My putter, please."

The king who got rooked. The King and Queen of Sweden drove to the ice arena in Lake Placid to watch the Swedish ice hockey team compete in the 1980 Olympics. The ticket-taker stopped the royal couple. Their tickets were for a different game.

The King explained that the correct tickets were in the car. "Could you make an exception for us, please?" he requested meekly. "You see, I'm the King of Sweden."

The ticket-taker laughed. "Sure you are, and I suppose this is the Queen?"

Rebuffed, the royal couple withdrew to fetch the correct tickets—too late. They saw their car being towed away for lack of proper identification.

Sitdown strike(out). Mary Ellen Magers of Pompono Beach, Florida, bowled 11 straight strikes and then put her twelfth ball into the gutter.

"Don't ask me why I did it," said Magers, 31, a professional bowler with a 205 average and a 300 sense of humor. "I was unbelieveably calm on the first eleven strikes. Then I interrupted my routine and sat down after the eleventh strike. All of a sudden I started to shake all over."

The ball hit her right ankle on the down swing and angled into the gutter before reaching the first arrows. She had to settle for a 290 game.

"I couldn't believe I could be so dumb," she moaned. "I guarantee you one thing. If I ever get to eleven strikes in a row again, I'm not going to sit down between strikes."

The gutter ball happened on September 25, 1980, and bestowed a unique distinction: the first woman ever to flub completely a chance for a perfect 300 game on the last ball.

Men are better at it. The American Bowling Congress listed 15 men who started with 11 strikes and then wasted the twelfth ball. Seven threw into the gutter and eight fouled.

All holds barred. Haverhill, Massachusetts, is the only city to outlaw female wrestlers by its own choice. The city council banned the ladies because "they undermine the dignity of womanhood."

Suds away. Sportsmen have challenged the English Channel in assorted and unusual craft. None can hold a rub-a-dub-dub to Bill Neal, 20, a British merchant seaman.

On August 10, 1981, Neal made the crossing in calm seas from Dover to Cape Griz Nez, France, in a steel bathtub. He used an oar as a paddle.

The tub, replete with faucets, was buoyed by layers of polystyrene to keep it afloat. The 21-mile trip took 31 hours and 29 minutes.

Better safe than sorry. When a visiting team of English cricketers refused to go through with a match in Jammu, India, in 1981, a mob of 3,000 burned down the main gate of the stadium. For five hours the visitors took refuge in their locker room while the mob hurled stones through the windows.

The visitors were English*women*, there to play a test against a side from the Indian Women's Cricket Association. An hour before the game they had surveyed the field and deemed it unsafe. The previous month a military parade featuring tanks had chewed the ground into a jagged tract of pits, ruts, and ridges.

Whopper of a blunder. Professional bowler Randy Lightfoot, of St. Charles, Missouri, had just won the 1978 Burger King Open in Miami, Florida. The smiling TV announcer asked the promotional question: Was he going to spend part of his $30,000 prize on Whoppers at Burger King?

"No," Lightfoot grunted.

The announcer grimaced, the audience shuddered, and members of the Professional Bowler's Association across the country had fits.

Burger King immediately suspended its sponsorship of bowling tournaments.

Predictions of things to come and came. The first 3:30 mile will be run in the year 2076. That's the forecast of David Rothman, director of a company named Analysis of Competitions and Tournaments.

Rothman revealed his formula. But . . . well, it's a trifle complicated. So let's move right along to Russia, where scientists predict the fastest man will soon cover 100 meters in 9:75. The ideal high jumper will leap 8'2".

Fine, only how long must sports fans wait?

Good news: not a second longer!

A record of the future has already been set. That's the opinion of Dr. Ernest Jokl of the University of Kentucky. He cited long jumper Bob Beamon's leap of 29'2½" at the 1968 Olympics.

Dr. Jokl called it a "mutation performance." It wasn't due till sometime in the twenty-first century.

So, he's not all thumbs. Old age finally caught up with Hai Deng, a Chinese Kung Fu master. The Peking newspaper, *China Daily,* reported that as a youth Hai Deng could balance himself upside down on one finger for two hours. In 1982, at the age of 78, he needed to use a finger and a thumb.

Watch your tongue. Female soccer players in Derby, England, managed to offend the gentlemen who refereed their games. So in 1973 officials began training women as referees.

Explained a spokesman: "Although the ladies' keenness is commendable, [male] referees who officiate at their matches rarely want to do so again. . . . The language can be quite startling."

Computer spare room. Executives at the Sandia Laboratory in New Mexico, one of the government's top-secret weapons labs, blew up when they checked the information storage banks of a company computer. Employees were using it to store the bowling team roster and the scores.

All fired up. In 1970 Gary Muhrcke, 39, a retired fireman on a full disability pension from an on-the-job back injury, entered the first New York City marathon. He won in the time of 2:31.

The disabled fireman had also entered the first race up the stairs of the Empire State Building—86 floors to the observation desk. He won that one, too.

Asked how he could run vertically and horizontally so far and so fast and yet not be able to work, Muhrcke answered, "Hey, I can run. I just can't lift."

Leslie, you coulda made us proud. When the women's liberation movement was at its height in the late 1970s, *The New York Times* appointed its first female sports editor. Stories about women athletes blossomed, sometimes to the point of wonder.

According to the *Times,* no woman ever achieved such an astounding triumph over male competitors as did Leslie Sewall of Plymouth, Massachusetts. In a one-column headline on June 1, 1980, the newspaper proclaimed:

MASSACHUSETTS WOMAN
TAKES WEIGHT-LIFTING TITLE

Sewall won the 114-pound national AAU title, beating a field of the country's top men. Reported the *Times:* "Miss Sewall, the lightest lifter in the competition at 50.9 kilograms, had a snatch of 82.5 and a clean and jerk of 100."

Those are championship lifts.

Sewall was proud of the lifts but couldn't have been too happy about the editorial change of sex that made "her" the strongest woman in the world. Leslie Sewall was a man.

By George! In 1982, 28-year-old Trevor George of Penarth, Wales, named his baby daughter after 20 of the world's leading soccer players.

The baby's multiple moniker: Jennifer, Edson Arentes do Nascimento (Pelé), Jairzinho, Rivelino, Carolos-Alberto, Paulo Cesar, Bretner, Cruyff, Greaves, Charlton, Best, Moore, Ball, Keegan, Banks, Gray, Francis, Brooking, Curtis, Toshack, Law George."

111

His wife sat down, wept, and went home to mother.

"I never expected him to give a girl those names," said the tot's mother, Lynette George. She had the baby's name legally changed to plain Jennifer Anne George.

"I'm more angry about her changing the names than about her leaving," grumbled George.

A turn for the worse. The pace-car driver of a 10-kilometer race in Detroit in 1981 took a wrong turn, torturing the 3,000 runners with an extra half-mile.

ABOUT THE AUTHOR

DONALD J. SOBOL, a once-upon-a-time baseball player, ducked behind the Fifth Amendment when urged to include some of his own athletic feats in this book.

As author of the highly acclaimed Encyclopedia Brown books, Mr. Sobol has received the Pacific Northwest Reader's Choice Award for *Encyclopedia Brown Keeps the Peace* and a special Edgar from the Mystery Writers of America for his contribution to mystery writing in the United States.

Donald Sobol is married and has three children. A native of New York, he now lives in Florida.

ABOUT THE ILLUSTRATOR

TED ENIK is a playwright, set designer, magazine artist, and cartoonist as well as a children's book illustrator. He is the illustrator of *Bob Fulton's Terrific Time Machine* by Jerome Beatty, Jr.; the Sherluck Bones Mystery-Detective books by Jim and Mary Razzi; the Slimy's Book of Fun and Games series by Jim Razzi; and several books in Bantam's Choose Your Own Adventure series, including *The Curse of Batterslea Hall, The Creature from Miller's Pond,* and *Summer Camp.* Mr. Enik lives in New York City.

Match Wits with America's
Sherlock Holmes in
Sneakers

ENCYCLOPEDIA BROWN

With a head full of facts and his eyes and ears on the world of Idaville, meet Leroy (Encyclopedia) Brown. Each Encyclopedia Brown book contains 10 baffling cases to challenge, stymie and amuse young sleuths. Best of all, the reader can try solving each case on his own before looking up the solution in the back of the book. "BRIGHT AND ENTERTAINING. . . ."
The New York Times
By Donald Sobol

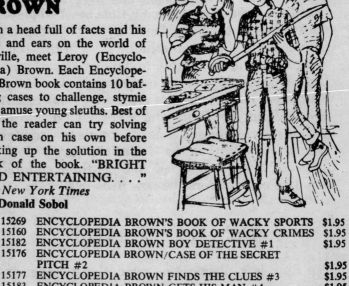

☐	15269	ENCYCLOPEDIA BROWN'S BOOK OF WACKY SPORTS	$1.95
☐	15160	ENCYCLOPEDIA BROWN'S BOOK OF WACKY CRIMES	$1.95
☐	15182	ENCYCLOPEDIA BROWN BOY DETECTIVE #1	$1.95
☐	15176	ENCYCLOPEDIA BROWN/CASE OF THE SECRET PITCH #2	$1.95
☐	15177	ENCYCLOPEDIA BROWN FINDS THE CLUES #3	$1.95
☐	15183	ENCYCLOPEDIA BROWN GETS HIS MAN #4	$1.95
☐	15180	ENCYCLOPEDIA BROWN KEEPS THE PEACE #6	$1.95
☐	15175	ENCYCLOPEDIA BROWN SAVES THE DAY #7	$1.95
☐	15181	ENCYCLOPEDIA BROWN TRACKS THEM DOWN #8	$1.95
☐	15178	ENCYCLOPEDIA BROWN SHOWS THE WAY #9	$1.95
☐	15184	ENCYCLOPEDIA BROWN TAKES THE CASE #10	$1.95
☐	15173	ENCYCLOPEDIA BROWN & THE CASE OF THE MIDNIGHT VISITOR #13	$1.95

Prices and availability subject to change without notice.

Buy them at your local bookstore or use this handy coupon for ordering:

Bantam Skylark Paperbacks
The Kid-Pleasers

Especially designed for easy reading with large type, wide margins and captivating illustrations, Skylarks are "kid-pleasing" paperbacks featuring the authors, subjects and characters children love.

☐	15258	BANANA BLITZ Florence Parry Heide	$2.25
☐	15259	FREAKY FILLINS #1 David Hartley	$1.95
☐	15250	THE GOOD-GUY CAKE Barbara Dillion	$1.95
☐	15239	C.L.U.T.Z. Marilyn Wilkes	$1.95
☐	15237	MUSTARD Charlotte Graeber	$1.95
☐	15157	ALVIN FERNALD: TV ANCHORMAN Clifford Hicks	$1.95
☐	15253	ANASTASIA KRUPNIK Lois Lowry	$2.25
☐	15168	HUGH PINE Janwillen Van de Wetering	$1.95
☐	15188	DON'T BE MAD IVY Christine McDonnell	$1.95
☐	15248	CHARLIE AND THE CHOCOLATE FACTORY Roald Dahl	$2.50
☐	15174	CHARLIE AND THE GREAT GLASS ELEVATOR Roald Dahl	$2.50
☐	15317	JAMES AND THE GIANT PEACH Roald Dahl	$2.95
☐	15255	ABEL'S ISLAND William Steig	$2.25
☐	15194	BIG RED Jim Kjelgaard	$2.50
☐	15206	IRISH RED: SON OF BIG RED Jim Kjelgaard	$2.25
☐	01803	JACOB TWO-TWO MEETS THE HOODED FANG Mordecai Richler	$2.95
☐	15034	TUCK EVERLASTING Natalie Babbitt	$2.25
☐	15268	THE TWITS Roald Dahl	$2.25

Prices and availability subject to change without notice.

Buy them at your local bookstore or use this handy coupon for ordering:

Bantam Books, Inc., Dept SK, 414 East Golf Road, Des Plaines, Ill. 60016

Please send me the books I have checked above. I am enclosing $_____ (please add $1.25 to cover postage and handling). Send check or money order—no cash or C.O.D.'s please.

Mr/Mrs/Miss _____

Address _____

City _____ State/Zip _____

SK—11/84

Please allow four to six weeks for delivery. This offer expires 5/85.

Here are more of the "kid-pleasing" paperbacks that everyone loves.